SMALL GROUPS:
TIMBER TO BUILD UP GOD'S HOUSE

BOB & WIN COUCHMAN

SMALL GROUPS

TIMBER TO BUILD UP GOD'S HOUSE

Harold Shaw Publishers
Wheaton, Illinois

Bible quotations, unless otherwise stated, are from Good News for Modern Man (TEV).

Copyright © 1982 by Bob & Win Couchman

Library of Congress Cataloging in Publication Data

Couchman, Bob.
  Small groups.

  1. Church group work.   2. Small groups.
I. Couchman, Win.   II. Title.
BV652.2.C68   259'.7   82-798
ISBN 0-87788-097-2 (pbk.)   AACR2

90   89   88   87   86   85   84   83   82

10   9   8   7   6   5   4   3   2   1

Printed in the United States of America

We dedicate this book to the people
we meet with Wednesday night in
Dick and Judy's living room.

CONTENTS

Preface

This is a book about small groups. Throughout the book we use this term to describe a group of people from one local church, meeting in their own neighborhood or community, that contributes to the life of that church.

A small group is not a church; it is part of a church. It is not an "interest" group. That is, it is not composed of persons who share a professional or avocational interest. Nor is it a peer group, embracing people from just one age segment or even one generation.

To us, a small group means a group of people, part of one congregation, living close to one another, who want themselves, others, and their church to be built up according to God's blueprint.

A small group, in the sense we are using the term,

might also be called a growth group, a neighborhood group, a cell group, *koinonia* group, a household or living-room group, or, in the picturesque old term, a cottage group.

In Haggai 1, God is explaining to his people why nothing is going right for them. He says: "Give careful thought to your ways. Go up into the mountains and bring down timber and build the house, so that I may take pleasure in it and be honored." We paraphrase. "Give careful thought to your ways of doing things. Consider meeting together in your living rooms to bring back timber to build up God's house."

We believe that small groups, as part of the local church, are, indeed, timber to build up God's house.

Foreword

Blessed is the pastor whose congregation includes Bob and Win Couchman. What he preaches they perform. They are models, living illustrations of all that he longs to see reproduced in the fellowship of believers.

They model marriage. In a society which has abused itself by its abuse of marriage, they present a winsome alternative, a solid, loving partnership.

They model mutuality. They are known as "the Couchmans"; they are referred to as "Win and Bob." They differ dramatically in temperament and in gifts but they lean hard on each other, draw from each other, encourage and support each other, and as a result, nourish each other into a wholeness of beauty.

They model maturity. Not the "we have arrived" caricature, but the genuine maturity that is dynamic and changing, growing and always moving upward. Open to ideas, eager to hear differing opinions, endlessly listening, ready to change but immovable from points of solid conviction, they show up shallowness and challenge superficiality.

They model ministry. Scarcely a week goes by without someone sharing what the Couchmans did for them. A fragile homosexual, a distraught mother, a pregnant teenager, a deserted husband. Their house is a home, a hospital, a haven, a taste of heaven for the hurt and the helpless. They teach creatively, they counsel patiently, they study assiduously, they give unceasingly. Everybody in the church knows of them, and amazingly, they seem to know most of the people. Their ears are open to hear problems but their mouths are closed. Their load is heavy, their burdens backbreaking, but their demands and requests are few.

When we launched our Neighborhood Group program with its attendant dissenters, disparagers, and doomsdayers, the Couchmans—surprise, surprise—were promptly committed and immediately involved. This book is a fragment of the story of their experiences as they have lovingly nurtured a group of people in their neighborhood so that they might become a reflection of the church of Christ in their square mile of responsibility. Challenged "to be the church" they gladly grasped the challenge, shouldered yet another responsibility, loaded more ministerial burdens on their backs, and by sheer leadership developed a caring, sharing community of believers.

If the church is *something that we are* rather than *somewhere that we go,* then the church is the Wins and

Bobs of this world who, when fed with the Word, burn up the calories of truth, and in the energy thus generated see the power of the Spirit released in holy living, corporate commitment, evangelistic zeal, missionary endeavor, and a host of good works. Blessed is the pastor of such a church. I should know, for I am that pastor and the Couchmans pastor me.

Stuart Briscoe

1

Why Have
Small Groups?

Picture this. It is Wednesday evening, 7:30. You have
come to church for the regular midweek meeting, and are
sitting about where you usually sit on Sunday morning.

In your mind's eye, rope off fifteen seats, putting your
seat in the middle of the three rows of five seats each.
Look to the left and notice the two people beside you. Look
to the right: two more. You really ought not turn around
to see who is behind you, but in front of you there is a bald
head and a greying head, a business man's neat haircut
and a woman's glossy red hair. You recognize all of these
heads, although the young fellow just sliding into the
seat at the end of that row is a stranger.

In your imagination re-enact the service. You are atten-
tive to the songleader who directs the congregation through

a hymn. You follow with interest the excellent Bible lesson which the pastor teaches. Then it is time to pray for one another. This goes slowly. The requests are primarily about health needs, and the people who pray are hard to hear. Some cannot be heard at all. A few of those praying proceed through the whole list of requests, and they seem to go on for a long, long time.

Now picture this. It is Wednesday evening, 7:00, a week later. The fifteen people who sat together last week in church have all gathered in a living room in your neighborhood. Because you all have a shorter distance to go, you are able to meet a half hour earlier than last week.

Scattered around the perimeter of the room on a couch, piano bench, rockers, dining-room chairs, and the floor, are the fifteen. In this oval seating arrangement you are all face to face.

The young fellow, the stranger, is cross-legged near you on the floor. You lean toward him, find out his name, and discover with delight that the flute beside him on the floor is, indeed, one he has brought along. The bald-headed gentleman unfastens his guitar case, and squats on the floor facing the flutist, inviting him to join him later in leading the singing. You leave the two musicians to discuss the evening's music, while behind you, you hear the hostess sliding open the stereo cabinet to reach the *High Praise* song books, which she passes around.

Meanwhile, other people have left their chairs to greet the flutist, hands are stretched across the room to grasp other hands. Some of the fifteen simply sit, and chat quietly, enjoying the unstructured moments—relaxed and at home.

The singing begins: fourteen voices, accompanied by

flute and guitar, are raised in praise to God. You lean back, close your eyes, and enter into the unashamed joy of worship.

During the Bible lesson time, everyone works from open Bibles. Many translations are used, and these add richness to readings and discussion. The lesson is a lively discussion under firm, purposeful leadership. Not everyone participates, but at least half of those present read, ask a question, or suggest an answer.

The business man is an eager participant. He is relatively new to all this, and full of questions, prefacing most with, "This is going to sound dumb, but. . . ." From the others come reassurances of, "No question is dumb," or "We all ask dumb questions" or "Hey, this is where we *all* get to ask our dumb questions."

After the lesson, it is time for prayer requests. Some who have been part of this group for a while are open about asking for prayer for their marriages, their hard hearts, their children, their faith. There is sharing of what God has been doing in situations that were prayed over in previous weeks. Everyone writes down the requests to be prayed over during the week. Now the requests, in summary form, are read aloud by a "regular." As each request is read, someone in the group raises his hand to acknowledge he will pray for that. Tonight the list is short, so each prayer need is prayed for out loud.

Finally everyone stands, stretching, and the patterns dissolve and re-form into clusters around the coffee pot, the couch, the doorway.

Compare the pictures
In the first picture, at the church, where was everyone

looking? How effective was the Bible teaching? The singing? What sorts of prayer requests were given? Was the
prayer time itself satisfactory? What was the level of
interraction between you and those seated around you?
What percentage of those at the church were able to
increase their spiritual skills through practice? What was
your opportunity to use your spiritual gifts, or other re-
sources, to serve?

Now, in your mind, change the picture to the one in the
living room and ponder the same questions.

While in the first situation, faces were all focused on the
front, in the second the entire group was face to face.
Probably the Bible teaching at the church was superior,
and maybe the singing also. However, the prayer was
more satisfactory in the living room, where more personal
requests were shared, and the discussion, with much
more participation, was lively and practical.

There was also a great contrast in the two settings, as
you considered the interraction between yourself and
those around you. In the small group, you felt more freedom to be yourself, and members could begin to discover
and practice spiritual gifts for the good of each other.

The place of the small in the large

A good local church is a place where people can come to
know Jesus Christ as their Lord and Savior and where
they can then grow as believers. It is a place to hear God's
Word and to begin to do what it says to do.

It is a bit like a course with two sections: a lecture
section and a laboratory section, and both sections are
required. James says: "Do not deceive yourselves by just
listening to his word; instead, put it into practice" (James

1:22).

On Sundays, the congregation in a good church hears the Word of God explained. This is a time to have one's Bible open and one's notebook handy. This is the lecture part of this essential course, and those taking the course need to pay strict attention to the lecturer and the Textbook.

On Sundays there ought to be growth through *hearing and accepting truth.*

But that is just half the course. There is still the learning and growing through *doing.* The adequate building up of ourselves and one another is nearly impossible in rows of pews, where eyes face front and silence is expected.

A useful part of the work of the church, then, can be for the congregation to break itself up into living-room-sized chunks during the week.

In the neighborhoods, neighbors meet to practice the course material. Here they have a chance to practice loving, serving, sharing, understanding, forgiving. Here also is one place where gifts of leadership of many kinds may be put into on-the-job training.

This concept, of small groups enriching the work of the church, is not new. Many years ago such meetings were popular, and were often referred to as "cottage meetings." Cottage meetings were characterized by frank dealing with matters too personal or time-consuming to be dealt with in the church proper.

Now, once again, many Christians are realizing that the work of the ministry is to be done by all of us. The biblical picture of the church is that of a body in which each member has a function. This is the body of our Lord Jesus Christ, and its members are all those who have personally received him through accepting his death for their sin. For the health and growth of the whole, we all must do our part. This involves finding out what we are capable of doing, practicing our growing skills, and becoming mature servers.

The pastor's responsibility, during his "lecture" time, is to open God's Word to us under the empowering of his Spirit. We need him to teach us truth about God, truth about how we ought to live for him.

And then we need an opportunity to take the truth we have been taught and begin to practice it. We need to learn, both by hearing and by doing. Together, these two parts of a church's life complement and enhance each other.

But how does it really work?

We have been leading such a group for over seven years. Wednesday night is a honey-sweet center in our week. As we write, it is a Thursday morning, and we recall last evening's meeting.

On Monday, one of the young wives called to say that she and her husband were becoming frustrated because of the lean spiritual content of their lives. They had become conscious of this shallowness on Sunday morning as the pastor spoke on marriage. She asked for help.

So last night we abandoned our regular study and we (Win and Bob) demonstrated our own mutual devotional life before the group. First we held hands and interviewed each other about our needs. Then we prayed for each other, for our children and for a few other needs, being as brief as possible, but seeking for a genuine re-enactment of our prayer time.

Then we did a Bible study together, using our Bibles and a study book. We had not rehearsed, wanting to share with these beloved neighbors the reality of our devotions.

We explained something of our devotional history, its long struggles and gradual growth. Then we sent everyone off, couples together and singles in pairs, to practice. Later we walked around, observing. There were Brent and Anita in the corner of the dining room, having such a good time studying (busy young high school teacher and busy young wife-mother-working person). Tom and Jessie were in a huddle at the kitchen table, murmuring. Carl and Lucy had taken over the family room and were deep into a serious discussion. And in twos throughout the rest of the house people quietly studied and prayed together.

Later Lucy commented: "It is one thing to be taught what you should do. It is quite another to have it acted out in front of you and then be led through doing it yourself."

The pastor had spoken strong truth on Sunday morning. It caught like burrs in the young couple's heart. Knowing we would be together Wednesday night, they had called us for help. We shared our own patterns and struggles without embarrassment, in an intimate setting. Then everyone in the group got a chance at a "lab experiment" and we all grew.

Summary
☐ Small groups change the focus from congregation/pastor to person/person.
☐ Small groups reduce the scale from the church sanctuary size to living room size. You come face to face, and close.

☐ Small groups make possible the involvement of many people in finding, practicing, and using ministry gifts at the same time. (While your group is singing and worshiping and sharing, so are many other groups from your congregation.)

☐ Small groups offer a more personal, intimate atmosphere in which one can feel "found" and interpersonal relationships can flourish.

☐ As acquaintances deepen into mutual trust and commitment, openness, vulnerability, and trust are natural developments; so burdens may be acknowledged and shared.

☐ The small group lends itself to informality; questions may be asked and answered; discussion seems natural. It is also a place where laughter and tears may appropriately be shared.

☐ As the participants in a small group feel increasingly at home, a less self-conscious atmosphere enriches their worship.

☐ A small group is like a heart. Into the heart, mid-week, straggle all the "tired blood cells" to get revitalized. Then out they pour, to share their vigor in the name of Jesus Christ.

It was he who gave some to be apostles, some to be prophets, some to be evangelists, and some to be pastors and teachers, to prepare God's people for works of service, so that the body of Christ may be built up until we all reach unity in the faith and in the knowledge of the Son of God and become mature, attaining to the whole measure of the fullness of Christ.

Then we will no longer be infants, tossed back and

forth by the waves, and blown here and there by every
wind of teaching and by the cunning and craftiness of
men in their deceitful scheming. Instead, speaking the
truth in love, we will in all things grow up into him who
is the Head, that is, Christ. From him the whole body,
joined and held together by every supporting ligament,
grows and builds itself up in love, as each part does its
work (Eph. 4:11-16 NIV).

Questions for study & discussion

1. Consider your own local church. Think about and
describe the atmosphere, growth, geographical distribu-
tion of the members, variation of ages, economic levels,
and lifestyles of the congregation. How would a small
group ministry meet two or three specific needs that you
see in the life of your church?

2. Do you think some people or groups of people in your
own church might be uncomfortable in the face-to-face
environment of a living-room group? Who would be uncomfortable? Why?

3. Discuss what a leader of a small group might do to
minimize the threat to persons coming for the first time.
Dramatize through role play the arrival of a shy new
person arriving for the first time, and a person from a
foreign culture. Have people take the part of the host/
hostess, leader, and the persons sitting beside each of the
newcomers. Discuss both the feelings each person had as
they acted out the role, and ways to make a group easier
to enter.

4. If small groups were to start in your local church,
what would be the most appealing way to publicize them?
In the past, what has been the most effective way to

present a new idea in your church? Brainstorm for the ways to attract people's interest in such involvement.

2
What Goes On in Small Groups?

Great-grandma Couchman was a very tiny lady, and as she grew older she compacted into something less than five feet in height, and that five feet was sorely infirm. Reaching things became a grave problem.

Then someone gave grandma a marvelous gadget: a long handle equipped with a "grabber" activated by a lever. The gadget leaned against her chair next to her cane, and when she dropped a spool of thread or a ball of yarn, she picked up the handle, hovered it over the dropped object and pulled the lever. The grabber grabbed, and the lost object was retrieved. That gadget greatly lengthened grandma's arm. Small groups are hands and feet and time and love at the end of a lengthened church body. They are good "grabbers" in neighborhoods.

A pattern from Peter

In the first letter bearing his name, Peter tells the believers
he is writing to

be clear-minded and self-controlled so that you can
pray. Above all, love each other deeply, because love
covers over a multitude of sins. Offer hospitality to one
another without grumbling. Each one should use whatever gift he has received to serve others, faithfully administering God's grace in various forms. If anyone
speaks, he should do it as one speaking the very words
of God. If anyone serves, he should do it with the strength
God provides, so that in all things God may be praised
through Jesus Christ. To him be the glory and the
power for ever and ever. Amen (1 Pet. 4:7b-11 NIV).

Peter was writing to members of the young Christian
church. They were experiencing many difficulties from
forces outside and inside their church. In this short passage of his letter, Peter seems to concentrate on interpersonal relationships within the church, as he gives them
very practical counsel on their attitudes and conduct. It is
helpful to remember that he was addressing people who
were meeting in homes. The home was the only church
building for these earliest Christians.

First, Peter directs the believers to be "clear-minded
and self-controlled so that you can pray." Among the
people who attend a small group, you will always find
those who are having trouble being clear-minded and
those who are struggling with self-control.

As such a group is maturing, people can begin to share
their problems there. Perhaps someone is having difficulty
thinking through a decision. His mind seems not to be

functioning clearly. People may come who have just had a death, who are being divorced, who have had police come looking for a child or a spouse, or who have lost their jobs.

People will come who do not know if they are in the right job, if they ought to go back to school, and so forth. Your group can meet a real need by praying for these people.

Another common category of need that will be shared in a group that is building trust is the need for self-control. At last, here is a place where people may dare to admit that they are over-eaters, that they have a sharp tongue, or that they have a problem with alcohol or anger.

A small group is a place where people can find prayer help for many, many needs, among them being the need for clear minds and self-control.

Above all: love

Next, Peter exhorts, "Above all, love each other deeply, because love covers over a multitude of sins."

The Greek word here translated by "deeply" is a word that means to stretch, to extend. It brings us right back to grandma's gadget. We are, above all, to learn to stretch our love further, to extend it.

A woman walks into a group and admits she has a drinking problem. She knows the Lord, and she is being hindered in her prayer life because of this problem. The group extends itself to love her by reaching out to her with prayer.

Once, in the beginning year of our group, we all became aware that a faithful attender had a drinking problem. We could smell the alcohol and hear the liquor's effect on the man's speech, week after week. Nothing was said.

Several months later, as the Bible study was about to begin one evening, the man interrupted in a very authoritative tone, "Hold it. Before we begin, I have a question to ask. Has someone in this group been praying about my drinking?" We all stared at him, stunned. One by one we admitted we had been praying about his drinking. But none of us had discussed it with anyone else in the group. As we stared at him, wondering what was coming, his face suddenly relaxed into a beautiful grin. "I was just wondering whom to thank," he said. "I have quit drinking." The room exploded in joy.

It was our first big adventure in stretching our love to cover someone's sins in prayer and in discretion. We have learned that God's Spirit commands us not only to love each other as we are today, but also to pray for one another's self-control, wisdom, and other needs, and to cover one another's weak areas and sin areas with love. We have a standing rule that nothing that is discussed in our group is ever to be mentioned outside the group. When we leave, we put the lid on what has been shared.

Spills don't count

"Offer hospitality to one another without grumbling," Peter continues. Small groups necessitate the weekly practice of hospitality. Hospitality, as a practical expression of stretching love, produces the climate in which spiritual growth can happen.

The welcome at the door, the preparations for the comfort of the people throughout the evening, the warm leave-takings are like a thermostat set on "comfort."

What positive word might we use to describe the phrase

"without grumbling"? Perhaps "wholeheartedly"? "Offer hospitality to one another wholeheartedly." A healthy group, that keeps on meeting far past a period of novelty, needs a reliable hospitality thermostat set at the comfort level.

Five years ago, when we were invited to move our sprawling youth group into a home, we visited the home to see if this really was God's plan for us. We walked into an attractive living room with a plush gold carpet. As we pictured forty to eighty kids sitting on the floor Saturday nights, our hearts sank. We glanced at each other doubtfully. Immediately, the sensitive woman who lived there said, "Spills don't count."

Five years later, that family's hospitality is still wholehearted. Nothing is ever mentioned about the extra cleaning, the furniture rearrangements fifty-two weeks of the year, the setting aside of family plans. We are welcomed home there each week, and although we will try to be careful, we still know that spills don't count.

Gifts are for sharing

One of the greatest potentials in a neighborhood group is realized when it acts as fertile ground in which the explanation, discovery, training, growth, and use of spiritual gifts can take place. Peter concerns himself with the use of gifts in passage quoted previously. "Each one should use whatever gift he has received to serve others, faithfully administering God's grace in various forms" (1 Pet. 4:10 NIV).

Each one is supposed to use the gift he has received, and he is supposed to use it to serve others. The New Testament clearly teaches that when a person trusts Jesus

Christ for salvation and accepts the forgiveness of his sins, he is given something special of God's choosing for the health and building up of the whole body of believers.

The gifts of the Holy Spirit are a little like zucchini. If you plant zucchini in your vegetable garden, it is hard to plant just enough for yourself. You always have extra to give away. In each of our lives, once we find new life in Christ, there begins to emerge at least one place where we ourselves are especially delighted and useful to one another.

One member of the group may find that prayer for the people in his group is becoming a responsibility and a joy that he takes more and more seriously. For someone else, there is deep pleasure in picking up a nondriver week after week. In God's genius plan for gifts, it may even be that the nondriver is the very one with the prayer gift, and that his prayer list begins with the person who takes him weekly.

As we discover our gifts and use them to serve each other, we also learn to face the fact that we, personally, do not have some gifts. Some of us cannot sing; some cannot teach. We are learning the truth of what Paul wrote: "Now the body is not made up of one part but many. If the foot should say, 'Because I am not a hand, I do not belong to the body,' it would not for that reason cease to be part of the body. . . . As it is, there are many parts but one body" (1 Cor. 12:14-15, 20 NIV).

Speaking the very words of God
One of the important gifts for the life of a small group is the gift of teaching. Such a group is not just a Bible study group, but Bible study is an essential part of it. This

teaching must be done by someone with a teaching gift, prayerfully and under the direction of God's Spirit, in order that whoever teaches does so "as one speaking the very words of God."

The ideal leader for these groups is a godly person who knows how to teach rather than lecture. This person needs to be knowledgeable enough about the Word of God so that he/she may act as a discussion leader and a resource person to keep the lesson, comments, and questions centered in truth.

The study materials used in the group may be quite simple or more advanced, the type of study being dictated by the needs of the entire group. The godliness of the teacher-leader and the recognized motive of growth for everyone are more important than the level of study.

God must provide the strength to serve

"If anyone serves, he should do it with the strength God provides, so that in all things God may be praised through Jesus Christ" (1 Pet. 4:11b NIV).

Rick and Karen led a group from their church. Seeking that in all things God might be praised, they chose a very simple Bible study, which Rick taught. When his church began a leadership training course as part of the Sunday school adult curriculum, Rick joined. He was serious about "faithfully administering God's grace." When he finished the course, he recommended it to several other persons in the group, and they enrolled.

Rick invited them, after they finished the course, to begin to do some of the teaching. And since he had chosen a rather simple study guide, they were encouraged to give it a try.

In the meantime, the group members decided it would be a blessing to meet at all the homes, in turn. So they visited ten homes in succession. One of the host women shared that when she had moved into her home she had knelt on the bare floor and asked God that she might some day have a Bible study within those walls. Hospitality opportunities multiplied tenfold.

Then Rick and his wife came into a difficult time in their own lives. Now there was no strength from God for leadership. They asked the group to pick up the responsibilities they had been carrying until they would find God-provided strength once more. Other homes were ready to practice hospitality. Other leaders had been trained. Covering love stretched out over them, and they were given freedom to rest awhile.

To him be the glory

When Rick and Karen served with God's strength, they were performing an act of worship. They served so God might be praised. When the rest of the group gave them their freedom, that service was also an act of worship.

Earlier in his direction Peter said, "Above all, love." Perhaps we could now say, "Around and under and in all, worship." We must love and teach and serve in the power of the Holy Spirit, in order that God through Jesus Christ might be praised.

One of the deepest delights of our group is the realization that all we do there in God's strength and for his glory is worship. So we sing his praises, we tell him we love him, and we are learning to live our worship, too. "To him be the glory and the power forever and ever. Amen."

What happens in a small group?
☐ Prayer
☐ Love
☐ Hospitality
☐ Gift sharing
☐ Teaching
☐ Service
☐ Worship
☐ Growth

Questions for study & discussion
1. Think back over your experience in Christian groups. In the small groups you have been part of, pick one to focus on. In this group you are thinking about, which of the following elements were included?
☐ prayer
☐ teaching
☐ worship
☐ interaction (sharing)
☐ outreach
2. Which of these five elements were *emphasized?*
3. From the list above, which did you feel most comfortable being involved in? Which was the most difficult for you? It might be interesting to discuss why some aspects were easier for you than others.
4. Decide if you think each of the five items above is essential to build up small segments of the true Christian church. If you decide each one is essential, share one specific way in which practicing each of these in an intimate setting might contribute to growth.

Example: "If I were looking right at you, seeing your feelings, and getting to know you week by week, it would make my prayers for you much more real and heart-felt. I would not only hear your prayer request, I would see how you were feeling. This would make it much easier for me to pray right then and to remember to pray again. It would also be good for you to hear my prayer, and feel *my* feelings."

3

Who Will Lead?

He was young, blond, and good-looking—conspicuous among the rest of us midlifers. Intrigued, I put my plate down on the table across from him and sat down facing him. We were at the halfway point in a one-day leaders' conference.

"Hi there." I began, "I don't believe we've met." He grinned, stuck out a big hand and introduced himself. "Enjoying the day?" I inquired. "Yup," came the cheerful reply.

I asked him about his present leadership involvement. With poise he answered, "I'm not leading anything yet, but I expect to be soon. I accepted Christ about three weeks ago and he gave me the gifts of leading and teaching so I am going to lead and teach."

Hoping my gulp didn't show, I guessed, "You're about seventeen?" He nodded. "We have a Bible study and fellowship for people your age. Maybe you would like to come be with us for a while and put some roots down before you start teaching."

Instantly he answered. "No. I don't want to be in a group. I'm going to lead one."

I wonder where he is. It must be about eight years since we sat at lunch together. I have little doubt that he did have a gift of leadership. It showed in his poise, his authority, his ambition. But so much else is necessary for good leadership besides the gift of leadership.

Needed: maturity

Recently, one of the small group leaders in our area came to his pastor to announce that his group was disbanding. When the pastor inquired about the cause of the proposed break up, the leader said the members had been together too long, and were finding that they really didn't like each other anymore. The pastor encouraged them to stay together, commenting, "if Christians are together more than about an hour, they start to fray around the edges. They start acting like family. They quit 'playing church.' They may stop liking each other. Small group members, staying together over a long period, have to quit or *learn to love each other with God's love,* which is primarily concerned with the well-being of the other person regardless of his condition or reaction. This love that continues after liking has quit is necessary to form a real church."

Small group leadership demands that the leader be mature enough to continue leading and encouraging the group to stay together long after the novelty is gone.

Needed: servanthood

Jesus repeatedly placed before his followers the concept of leaders who serve. He both taught and modeled this idea. He said of himself that he came to serve and not to be served. Then to demonstrate that this was true, he served those to whom he had come as healer, banquet organizer, foot washer, comforter, and savior.

Paul, Jesus' follower, inspired by the Spirit of Jesus, continued both the teaching and the acting-out of this style of leadership. For example, he wrote to the young believers at Thessalonica reminding them that when he was with them he was as gentle among them as a mother feeding and caring for her own children. A recurring theme in his letters is his boast that he worked night and day in order not to be a burden to those he had come to help.

One of the good things about a small group is that there are so many opportunities for mutual service. There are chairs to carry and babies to hold. There are songbooks and cookies to pass around. There are sick people to visit and weddings to attend. The leader doesn't have to do it all. He cannot do it all. He mustn't do it all. But he sets the pattern.

From welcoming people as they come, to being obedient to the guidelines given him by his church, the small group leader leads his group into growth by serving.

Needed: leadership gifts

Leaders have to lead. The leader is responsible for not allowing his group to spin out of control or head in the wrong direction. Truth must be taught; guidelines must be kept; participation must be balanced and study goals achieved.

The people in the group need a leader with a quality that allows them to feel comfortable following him. The Holy Spirit gives to each personal Christian some special gift of usefulness to benefit the whole Body of believers. The leadership gift is one of these.

It is, in part, an inner authority. God's gift of leadership allows the one possessing it to lead, where appropriate, without manipulation, without a strident voice. Christian leaders ought to motivate people to do God's will, "not by might, not by power, but by my Spirit, says the Lord."

Because the gift of leadership is a powerful gift, it needs always to be exercised in constant leaning on the God who imparted it.

Needed: willingness to be oneself

When we began leading our neighborhood group, we were afraid someone would find out that we were failures as parents. Seven years ago we were at the tail end of our child-rearing years, and were feeling that we had never done anything right as parents.

One night, a few months after our group began, one of our regular members walked in, collapsed onto a chair and called out, belligerently, "Am I allowed to say that I am in pain, frustrated, terribly angry? Is this a place where I get to be honest, or isn't it?" As we all rushed to assure her that she could be honest, an important part of our life together was born.

Because of her example, the rest of us began to be more open. Bit by bit we all, including us leaders, tiptoed into honesty. We had started, in the pastor's words, "to fray around the edges, to quit playing church."

Not only do leaders need to be honest and thereby encourage honesty, they need to be themselves in the sense of going with their own style.

Bob is a wood person. He carves it, turns it, builds things with it, refinishes things made of it. He is enamoured of wood. In a light mood he created a series of panels for our front door. There are carved panels and framed assemblages and there is even a row of old wooden organ stops.

Who would have guessed that that door would be used by God to make hundreds of kids feel at home? In the 70s, as streams of young people began to come to our home to attend Bible studies, there were many newcomers each week.

We would watch them park down the street, approach the house with a tentative air, and finally knock. We tried to be right there to welcome them. Nearly always, the first thing they noticed was Bob's whimsical door. They would ask about it, running their fingers over it, and we would explain, pointing out odd little aspects of it they had missed.

By the time the door tour was complete, they were usually at ease enough to venture into the living room, ready to step over the other teens sitting on the floor to find a spot for themselves.

Our host family for our neighborhood group is avidly interested in tennis. Step into their family room, and you are nearly blinded by the glitter of all the trophies. The man of the house is a fine photographer and his work is framed and displayed throughout the house. The home where we meet with our young people on Saturday nights has sheltered many foster children over the years. Although all the children born and borrowed have grown and gone, everywhere you look, there are children's things: under a lamp table is a tiny doll's table set up for a party, teddy bears hiding in corners, and Christmas tree decorations swinging year round above the sink.

The leader's willingness to be personal, to be the "flavorful" person he is, enhances the sense of the specialness of each group.

Needed: God's love

Let's listen, again, to that pastor's definition of God's love: "Primarily concerned with the well being of the other person regardless of his condition or reaction. This love that continues after liking has quit is necessary to form a real church."

Who has that kind of love? It makes one groan to think of loving everyone who comes to a group, regardless of his condition or reaction, and continuing to love him month in and year out.

Paul asks, "Who then is capable for such a task?" He asks this question as he writes to the believers at Corinth, believers who gave Paul many heartaches. Then he answers his own question: "There is nothing in us that allows us to claim that we are capable of doing this work. The capacity we have comes from God. It is he who made us capable of serving the new covenant, which consists not of a written law but of the Spirit. The written law brings death but the Spirit gives life" (2 Cor. 3:5-6).

"The Spirit gives life." The leader who is going to love his people with God's love must be very dependent upon

God's Spirit. It is the Spirit of God who will keep the leader creative, flexible, accepting. Only God's Spirit will be able to keep him from despair or arrogance or possessiveness.

Needed: training
Leaders need to learn leadership skill. Leaders deserve to be trained. This is a responsibility that the church proper may wish to undertake.

Who is the leader?
The leader may turn out to be you. The leaders may be a couple. The leaders may be a team. There may be a host family and a teaching person or couple. A typical pattern would be for the group to have one person or couple in whom the leadership would reside. But as gifts and growth among the members are discovered and nurtured, the weight of leadership is often shared.

Three days ago a woman driving in from another state to inquire about small group leadership asked, "On a scale of one to ten, where would the leader have to be, as far as maturity and gifts go?"

Perhaps you are asking yourself if you are ready for the job. So let's summarize.

The leader of a small group needs to be:
☐ Becoming mature.
☐ Learning to be a servant.
☐ Endowed by God's Spirit with the ability to lead.
☐ Willing for his group to see his frailty.
☐ Honestly himself.
☐ Open to loving with God's love.

☐ Increasingly dependent upon God's Spirit.
☐ Trained.

Questions for study & discussion
1. As you think about the possibility of leading a small group, use the following questions to help decide if you are gifted with some leadership qualities:

☐ Make a list of anything you have been involed in as a leader.

☐ Have you had some success in leadership situations?

☐ How do you *feel* about being a leader? (Sick to your stomach? Excited? Fearful? Challenged? Eager? Nervous?

2. Can you name four ways that you have grown as a believer over the last five years? Think about things like your devotional life, your personal relationships and your Christian responsibilities for clues about your growth (see Heb. 5:11-14).

3. If you can see that you do have some leadership gift, and that you are really growing as a believer, the next thing to examine is what kind of skills would need training and sharpening to help you be a good leader.

☐ Would you need help in leading people to pray? In encouraging free and fruitful discussion? In teaching the Bible? In encouraging worship? In blending people so interaction takes place? In encouraging service?

4. Read through the sample lesson in the appendix of this book. Imagine yourself as the leader and discuss your reactions. What parts would be comfortable? What would be difficult?

5. Where could you get such training? Is it available in your church? Do you think it might be added to your church's Adult Education curriculum if there were sufficient interest?

4

What Will Be Taught?

Each week the leadership of your group gets to present the evening as a gift to the group. It is a gift given to them, by God, through you, the leader. Imagine holding out to them a good-sized box: a shoe box or a shirt box. Together you take the lid off, and inside are several small packages, each one a different shape, size and weight.

Let one of these imaginary inner boxes stand for worship, another for prayer. In this corner is the Bible teaching package, and in that corner is a group service project. The gift of the evening arrives in good shape because it has all been packaged in protective prayer.

Each part of the package is wrapped up in the growing love, trust, and interaction of the group life. This gift-wrap transforms everything it touches.

Surprises

Variety is like a surprise package. Sometimes the variety is in the order you do things; sometimes it is in the content of your time together.

At the end of this chapter there is a sample lesson. It happens to be the sort of lesson that might lead a group to apply what it had learned by worshiping together using the Bible material studied. If you, the leader/teacher, see this as a possibility, you may choose to worship after the lesson. So, although you usually have a time of praise at the beginning of your evening, there may be opportunities to worship at another time, and have that other time be more meaningful.

Variety of order, when appropriate, can freshen a group that has met together over a long period.

Varying the content of the agenda is another possible surprise package. Novelty, planned with prayer and sensitivity, can banish boredom. We have had ethnic meals and Thanksgiving feasts together. We end each summer with a corn roast. Our monthly "kids" night and neighborhood caroling are other special events that keep us out of a rut.

The particular circumstances of each group give opportunities for changes in routine, and the sensitive leader can take these and make use of them.

Recently we altered our regular routine to have a night of praying over a couple about to be married. The girl, Laura, had been part of our group for two years; Peter drove eighty miles to be there. We prayed for them and gifted them and celebrated their coming marriage in the warmth of the living-room sized group.

It is easy to slide into the pattern of having a single, pronounced emphasis of activity. We must continually check the gift box to see if we are putting into it only Bible study, or only praise, or only building relationships.

The activity of small groups must be broken down into the components that will help realize the group's purpose. Then, these components must all be included over a long period. It is not necessary to include them all at every gathering. Both variety and balance are essential to the health of each group.

The teaching package

Teaching will be a central part of most evenings. The teaching that is most appropriate for this sort of group is nearer guiding than preaching, nearer discussion than lecture. Remember, the leader should be like a "lab instructor." Whenever possible he needs to keep his own hands stuffed in his lab coat pockets, allowing and motivating the students to get their hands into the experiment. Yet he is the instructor. He is the leader. He is responsible to keep things headed in the right direction and to see that all in the group are working on the same "experiment." He needs to be an encourager, while being the instrument of the Holy Spirit to guide the group into all the truth.

Continuity

We freshen our group life with variety. We move toward the entire goal as we are careful to maintain a balanced content. A third essential quality is continuity. Group members would be discouraged if only new songs were sung every week. In the same way, it would be frustrating if unrelated lessons were the usual pattern for teaching.

It is wearying for the teacher to try to think of some new topic to teach each week. It is helpful to know ahead of time that there is a relationship between what one taught last week and what one will teach this week and in the weeks ahead. For the group members, those who are part of the group because they desire to mature, related lessons can become a grid of God's truth, into which they may increasingly place their lives. Discontinuous teaching diminishes the sense of life-flow, the sense of a personal group history.

Focus on Scripture

Returning to the analogy of the group as a laboratory, think of the teaching part of the evening as that time when a portion of Scripture is placed under the microscope. A study based on a book of the Bible, or a part of a book of the Bible, lends itself ideally to this concept. In this sort of study, group members are asked to observe the content with care, focusing simply on what is being said. They are identifying the content of a portion of truth. They are noticing who is in action, where the action is taking place, and what the action is. They become aware of the literary genre of this portion of Scripture. Is it poetry, narrative, history, admonition, or straight teaching?

After some time at this level of observation, the group begins to consider the meaning of what they have been reading. What does it mean? What principles are taught here, directly or indirectly?

When some understanding about meaning has been gained, the group members are ready to move onto the third step: What is it teaching them? How can they apply what has been identified and understood to their own lives? What should they do with what they have learned? What should their response be?

In a chemistry lab, the third step might be that time in which students would be asked to choose a project, making use of the materials they had observed, identified, and learned the uses of. The time has come to put what they have learned *to use*.

In a living room group, the third step involves putting into practical use the truth that has been discovered and grasped intellectually. The responsibility of the leader/ teacher is to help a group acquire skills of observation, of sorting out principles being taught, and then motivating it to apply those principles in practical ways.

The value of inductive Bible study

This three-step system—observation, meaning, and application—defines inductive Bible study. Its value for small groups is that it keeps a balance between hearing the Word and obeying it. Believers need both. Too much emphasis on intellectual understanding without personal application produces unhealthy Christians just as does diving into application without checking the anchor of God's Word.

Inductive Bible study respects the material itself. It attempts to discover or clarify the meaning of the Scripture rather than reading into it preconceived ideas. It forces us to observe the whole flow of a passage, rather than isolating a particular subject for us to focus on. Inductive Bible studies march bravely through a whole portion of truth, carrying those who follow along toward maturity.

To summarize
Each small group evening may be like a gift box, filled
with good things, packed in prayer, and wrapped in growing love. The inner contents of the box need to be chosen
with care, in order to supply variety, balance, and continuity.

Bible teaching characterized by continuity is desirable.
A special approach to Bible teaching called "inductive"
lends itself well to a series of studies in a book of the Bible.
Inductive Bible studies pose these questions:
☐ What does the text say?
☐ What does the text teach?
☐ How does the text apply to me?
The goal of the teaching aspect of a small group might be
stated in this way: to lead its participants to greater skills
in observing and understanding God's Word, and to deep-
en their desire to apply it.

P.S.—Special to teachers
There are many very good inductive small group Bible
study books available. Neighborhood Bible Studies (Tyn-
dale House), Fisherman Bible Studyguides (Harold Shaw
Publishers), and InterVarsity Small Group Bible Study
books (InterVarsity Press) are all excellent. Some of these
series actually teach, while others simply ask questions
without giving answers. Choose carefully, being aware of
your own needs as a teacher, and of the variety of levels of
expertise present in your group.

Carpenter Studyguides is a new series by Harold Shaw
Publishers designed particularly for small groups within
the church. Ideas for worship, prayer, interpersonal and
outreach ministry, as well as Bible study, are included.

(The Appendix at the back of this book contains a sample lesson from both the Member's Manual and the Leader's Handbook of *James: Hear It! Live It!,* a Carpenter Study-guide.)

5
Worship

More than 600,000 people jammed the mall, flowing into the area around Buckingham Palace, as they waited to see Charles, Prince of Wales, and his princess, on their wedding day. Keeping their eyes on the balcony, straining to catch the first glimpse of them appearing, the crowd roared, "We want Charlie! We want Charlie!"

Again I looked, and I heard angels, thousands and millions of them! They stood around the throne, the four living creatures, and the elders, and sang in a loud voice:

"The Lamb who was killed is worthy
to receive power, wealth, wisdom, and strength,
honor, glory, and praise!"

And I heard every creature in heaven, on earth, in the world below, and in the sea—all living beings in the

universe—and they were singing:
   "To him who sits on the throne and to the Lamb,
   be praise and honor, glory and might,
   forever and ever!" (Rev. 5:11-13)

"We want Charlie, we want Charlie! . . ." The British reserve gave way before the joy of the moment.

And in heaven one day, with all our reserve gone forever, we will abandon ourselves to eternal joy and shout and sing together, "Worthy is the Lamb! Worthy is the Lamb!"

As believers worship, they are rehearsing for that time when they will take their places in the crowd around the throne. Worship is giving God what he deserves. He deserves honor and glory and praise, and whether we give that to him on earth or in heaven, we give him what he richly deserves.

But to worship now is not merely to rehearse, or practice the normal business of heaven. While rehearsing, *we actually do it.* The child riding his first bicycle, pushed along down the driveway by his father, wobbling as he goes, may be clumsy, funny, embarrassed. But he is learning to ride his bike.

Worship is the most objective aspect of prayer. In worship we struggle to concentrate on who God is and what he has done. As we wrestle with thinking about him, we avoid thinking about ourselves. As we worship, we may feel clumsy, funny, embarrassed. But we are learning, and we are worshiping.

The people gathered around Buckingham Palace on Prince Charles's wedding day seemed to have forgotten for the moment such things as high taxes and unemployment. They were given over to being happy for the royal couple. They were absorbed in celebration.

Within a small group of people who have come together
to practice their Christianity, worship is a most important
activity. Although it may take a long while to begin to feel
free from the clumsiness and self-consciousness of a worship experience, God accepts the worship of his people
with joy. He is worthy of our adoration, and we need to get
on with expressing that. As we worship him, we are
reaching toward that level in our relationship to God in
which the self puts itself firmly to one side and concen-
trates on the object of worship. It is the highest level of
relating to God. When we worship we are doing what we
ought to do, we are pleasing God, we are maturing spiri-
tually, and we are getting ready to enjoy heaven, to cele-
brate the King.

Worship in spirit and truth

Jesus said to the Samaritan woman: "But the time is
coming and is already here, when by the power of God's
Spirit people will worship the Father as he really is, offer-
ing him the true worship that he wants. God is Spirit
and only by the power of this Spirit can people worship
him as he really is" (John 4:23-24).

Nearly a billion people are said to have watched the
royal wedding in person or on television. Why did people
bother to sleep out in the parks of London, or get up before
dawn in America? They wanted to see the procession, the
ceremony, the couple.

One of our chief difficulties as Christians is not seeing
yet the one we are learning to adore. If we cannot see
what the Lord is like, however are we to worship him
truly?

In Jesus' comments to the woman of Samaria, we have

the answer. First of all, this passage in John comforts us
with the information that God is seeking worshipers.
That's reassuring. Next, he reminds her and us that God
is Spirit. That looks like a problem. We wish he were
Spirit housed in a body we could see. It is a great help to
remember that he once was in a body: the body of our
Lord, Jesus Christ. It is a great help to know that his
Spirit has taken up residence in each one of us who is
born of God. But still, we long to see him. We would wrap
ourselves up in a blanket in the park; we would be the first
one to get up before dawn, if only we could see him.

Jesus continues speaking: "Only by the power of his
Spirit can people worship him as he really is." There is
our assignment. We are at this time living by faith and
not by sight. We have God's Spirit to help us, and by the
power of his Spirit we can worship him as he really is,
even before we see him.

God reveals himself as he really is in the Scripture.
There are almost endless descriptions of himself that he
gives us in his Word. As we read these descriptions a
picture, an outline of God, grows clearer to our inward
eye. His Spirit takes this truth and makes it real to us. Our
inner vision of God takes on substance, weight, life.

During Bible study, we learn truth. During worship, we
take the raw material of the truth and the Spirit of God
makes it real to us and we are able to praise God as he
really is.

Worshiping together
In a group of believers who are growing to trust one
another, the worship of each one can help to ignite the
praise flame in another. We would like to share here some

living-room-tested ideas for corporate worship in a small group.

Praise from the Psalms
Have everyone turn to the book of Psalms in their Bibles. Give each person time to find a verse of praise for who God is or what he has done. When everyone has found a verse, ask each to share. (We have found it helpful to let people share in any order, or not to share at all. "Going around the room to the right" means that all must participate.) Ask that the people not add the reference, but simply read the verse. Let this be leisurely. Encourage people to listen to each verse. Do not be afraid of silence.

When as many people as desire to do so have read, ask anyone who is comfortable in doing so to restate his verse in his own words, putting it into the first person, and praying it back to God.

For example, Psalm 107:1 states "Give thanks to the Lord because he is good: his love is eternal!" Stated personally and as a prayer, one might say: "Thank you Lord that you are one hundred percent good. Your goodness makes all the difference as I try to trust you. Another thing that makes all the difference is that your love never stops. Remembering that there is nothing but goodness in you, and that your love never gives up, I feel very, very secure. Amen."

In many of the Psalms, the instructions are given to praise God in song. When we use the Psalms as the basis for worship, we like to intersperse our reading and speaking of praise with our sung praise.

We have been using *High Praise* (Harold Shaw Publishers), and appreciate the fact that all of its songs are purely Scripture set to music. When we are singing our worship, we choose those songs which express praise. Our group knows many praise choruses by memory, and we use these, too, during worship.

Praise based on who God is
Ask each person in the group to think of a title or one-word description of God. (If the group is larger than ten or twelve persons, have people team up to do this.) Examples of titles or descriptions would be Creator, Shepherd, Lamb, Door, and so on. The leader might suggest just one example to be sure the group is understanding what is wanted.

When everyone has decided on a word, have someone make a written list of all the words chosen. Then pile several concordances in the middle of the floor. Invite people to find a verse that uses the word for God that they have chosen. Some of your group will probably know where to find such a verse, but some may not. Explain the use of a concordance, being careful not to take for granted that everyone knows how to use one.

Give everyone enough time to find a verse, and to report the reference to the person who has made a list. (It may be that someone will discover he cannot find that word used in the Bible. Encourage such a person to choose another word. At this point, the leader may remind everyone that we are to worship the real God, who has described himself in his Word. By checking chosen names for him against the Word, we limit ourselves to reality.)

After the references have been recorded, ask the persons, or the pairs, to pray, asking God's Spirit to make real to them the facet of God's character or activity that they have chosen. (This is private, or paired-prayer, not group wide.)

Suggest that after they pray, they reread their verse, ponder what the verse and especially the name in the verse reveal to them about God. They may want to close their eyes and visualize God as Creator, creating all the planets, or as Shepherd, leading everyone in the group, etc. If the people are working in pairs, they can, at this point share their impressions with their partner. This will be difficult for some peole, so be sensitive to the amount of time given them to meditate on God in this way.

Then invite people to: 1) share their name for God; 2) read aloud the verse containing the name; and 3) describe their thoughts or mental picture as they have meditated on their verse.

Then ask people to pray briefly, addressing God by the name they have been working with, and praising him for that aspect of his character or activity. Let people pray or abstain. Never force praise.

In our experience using this method of worship with our group, there was a slow start to the sharing of meditations and praise, as people felt a little self-conscious. However, each person's contribution seemed to spark one from someone else. There seemed to be a grouping of names of God and related sharing and praise. "Friend" was followed by "Companion," and "Powerful God" came on the heels of "The God Who Provides."

Other worship matters

Do not attempt to create a certain mood of worship. It is important not to manipulate the mood of a group. There are many different sorts of atmospheres in which praise may flourish. There may be deep quiet, laughter, shouting or whispering. Let God choose.

How long should a small group take for worship? The "package" marked "Worship" in the gift box of each evening may vary. Recently, when we used the *Praise based on who God is* plan, we had time for worship and intercessory prayer and then it was time for coffee. Yet individual Bible study was a large part of this particular worship plan. The use of the concordances helped people become accustomed to this most basic of Bible study tools. We hooked our worship deeply into Bible truth. We meditated on truth. We asked the Spirit to give us power to praise the real God on the basis of that truth.

Our group seemed refreshed by turning away from its owns needs first. Then it was good to come back to prayer for each other. The order felt right. The emphasis on praise cheered our spirits.

Service as worship
Worship is what we give God because he is worthy of it. The English word "worship" was originally "worthship." We give our lives to him because he has bought us with his blood. That is our first act of worship. We worship him as we sing praises to him and learn about him and talk to him and clap our hands in celebration of him. But we also worship him as we serve each other in his name and for love of him.

Summary
In worship we must be helped by God's Spirit, informed by God's Word, encouraged by other believers around us as we remember that what we are all doing now we will be

doing forever: celebrating the King.
  "Worthy is the Lamb!"
  "Worthy is the Lamb!"

An adventure in worship

Psalm 103 is a good praise Psalm. In it, David encourages his inner man to praise God. Here is a suggestion for using this psalm as a group worship experience.

1. Read a phrase or verse of the psalm aloud. Stop and think what you have read. Let the words hang in the air. Meditate; then comment on what you have read. For example: verse 1 says, "Praise the Lord, my soul! All my being, praise his holy name!" You might comment, "I have never thought about what it means to praise God with all my being. I guess that would include things like my expression, the way I hold myself, what I wear. It is a new thought."

Or, instead of commenting, you may want to praise God directly, using the psalmist's words as your guide. For example, "God, one of your names that I want to praise you for is Creator. I love beauty and creativity. It excites me to remember that all beauty and creativity come from you. Thank you for making ice crystals on my window when the flowers in my garden die."

2. Allow all who wish to participate to do so.

3. At the end, discuss your feelings about God and each other as you have gone through Psalm 103 this way.

6
Prayer

Wouldn't it be terrible if all we had to offer each other for our great needs were wishes?

Imagine that you are at your regular group meeting and everything is as it has always been except that there is no such thing as prayer.

Dick: "I have something to share with everybody. I lost my job today. My boss walked into my office after lunch and informed me that my whole engineering group is out."

Hans: "I can't believe what you're saying. Didn't you just get an excellent report from him about your performance?"

Dick: "Unfortunately, that has nothing to do with it. Because of the economic situation, somebody higher up

decided that the number of groups has to be cut and for
several reasons that have nothing to do with me, ours
was the group that got it."

Judy: "I'm thinking right away about your family.
We've got to do something. Let me think. . . ."

Hans: "It isn't much, Dick, but I do offer you my sincer-
est sympathy and best wishes. I'll keep my ears open."

Judy: "My best wishes, too, Dick. I wish there were
something more I could do. This is so frustrating."

Others in the group: "We're really sorry, Dick." "Good
luck, Dick." "We'll really be thinking about you." "Keep
in touch, brother."

A wish is a pebble thrown by a child. A prayer is a
rocket launched. In faith, God's child prays in the name
of Jesus. The Spirit directs the prayer in accordance with
God's will and, in accordance with that will, God acts.

Our wishes cannot produce results. Our prayers? Listen: "By means of his power working in us [he] is able to
do so much more than we can ever ask for, or even think
of: to God be the glory in the church and in Christ Jesus
for all time for ever and ever! Amen" (Eph. 3:20-21).

Of course we are often unwise and always limited in
our prayers, but God helps us. "In the same way the Spirit
also comes to help us, weak as we are. For we do not know
how we ought to pray; the Spirit himself pleads with God
for us in groans that words cannot express. And God,
who sees into our hearts, knows what the thought of the
Spirit is; because the Spirit pleads with God on behalf of
his people and in accordance with his will" (Rom. 8:26-27).

"On behalf of his people . . . in accordance with his will."

In the name of the Son, our high priest, we come into
the presence of the Father with our petitions. Carrying

our simplest request and our deepest longings we enter
the throne room of heaven. The Spirit pleads with God on
our behalf, coming to our aid, because he sees we do not
know what to pray for. He interprets our prayers, bringing
them into alignment with the perfect will of the Father for
us.

Praying together

God does great things when believers pray, and members
of your group want to experience that together. But how
can people in newly formed groups gain courage to ask
for prayer and gain experience in effective praying for
each other?

Prayer reflects overall Christian maturity. In the beginning, each group is a baby group. As it grows in its
overall life, its prayer will grow in reality, content, and
intimacy.

Growth takes time. The leader, in his role as "lab instructor," must find ways to encourage and challenge
without being destructive.

Getting started

For several weeks after our group began meeting, we (Bob
and Win) did the praying. We began and ended our evenings with short prayers, asking God to be among us as
Teacher, and commending the group members to him.
We tried not to use a special vocabulary and tone of voice,
desiring simply to talk with our Father before our brothers
and sisters.

But in a very few weeks we sought ways to involve
more people. One evening after our Bible study, we asked
everyone to find a little piece of paper, and on that to write

a vital need. Folded and anonymous, the scraps formed a little heap in the middle of the floor. Then anyone who would commit himself to praying daily that week for a need was invited to pick up a note and take it home.

From that first group experiment we remember this. Our host picked up one note and read: "I want to have a baby." He stuck the note in the corner of his bedroom mirror and prayed over it as he combed his hair each morning. His children spotted it there and asked him why he wanted a baby. Several months later, a woman in the group asked who had gotten the prayer request about the baby. When the host acknowledged he had, she told him her story. For a long time she and her husband had wanted a child. Discouraged, they finally applied for a baby through an adoption agency. But before the arrangements for their adoptive child were complete, she found she was pregnant. How encouraged we all were.

From the notes we moved on to one-word thank-you prayers. After proper explanations, Win might begin with "Thank you Father for this warm room on this below-zero night." Others were invited to add single words to this. "Health," "stars," "children," "forgiveness," "love," . . . Slowly, thoughtfully, the single words hung like incense in the air.

For anything more than one word a living-room is too big a setting for group members' first audible prayers. But a living-room can become several smaller spaces if people sitting next to one another are invited to pray together over something specific. "Before we begin our lesson, maybe you and whoever is sitting next to you could ask God to help us understand what we are learning tonight. Pray out loud or silently. It is up to you."

Sometimes we sent people off in twos and threes to other rooms. The extra privacy helped.

Josie is from Switzerland. Her son, having found Christ on his university campus, shared him with his mother. Then he did some telephoning and found our group meeting near her home. So he brought Josie to us, before leaving for his first job out of the state. Josie has a delightful accent. But perhaps it was that very accent that made her shy about praying aloud. She would often come to us after the study time to apologize for not having talked or prayed. We tried to reassure her, but her silence persisted.

Jerry worked at the same firm as Josie, and both were very faithful in their attendance on Wednesday nights. One night Debbie, Jerry's wife, said she had come alone because Jerry was sick. That was too much for Josie. Her concern for Jerry proved stronger than her self-consciousness. During prayer time, without prompting from any of us she prayed: "And please, Lord, make Jerry well."

Each week our church sends us a sheet listing the prayer requests and praises that have been received in person, by letter, or phone. These include missionary requests. These lists, oddly, were both harder and easier to pray through than were our own requests. They were harder because many of them were about people we did not know. We were not personally interested. They were easier because we were not sharing our own needs; there was no embarrassment. We could ask God to please bring Mary's wandering husband home more easily than ask it for ourselves.

These church lists gave us a faint, but growing, church-wide concern. They also served as prayer examples. A young believer might discover here someone else praying over a hot temper or a university exam or something else that he had no idea was "proper" prayer material.

God was gracious in giving us a number of persons who had been believers a long while and who were at home praying aloud, as well as asking for prayer.

Besides all of these rather specific prayer development helps, we, ourselves, prayed over and worked at creating a tender environment for prayer. Although we often failed, we desired that this would be a setting in which people would not feel trampled or pushed, but open and quite secure.

Going on

Our patterns, always evolving, reflect our growing closeness. We care about each other, and this is evident even in our greetings: "Hi, everybody! Thanks for praying. Michael is ever so much better," or "Mary, how is your Mom? Everything OK?" Without thinking about it, we often begin our conversations with each other inquiring about something or sharing the answer to something that was prayed over the week before.

We usually end the structured time of our evenings with the intercession part of our prayers. Typically, someone keeps track of prayer requests as they are mentioned. We try to listen to these carefully and to ask questions until we feel we understand the requests. When we have received all requests, the list is read off and those who wish to, pick one to pray for. Then we pray aloud, in turn, but not in any set order.

When we have visitors who might be uneasy if subjected to an overlong session, or when our worship, sharing, or study has stretched too long, we vary our format. On those occasions we pray in the usual way but silently, so that we can all pray at the same time, or we each take our chosen request home to give it special attention there.

We also pray for each other during the week. We have a hot-line arrangement to be used for real crises. Otherwise, many of us have committed ourselves to praying for group needs on different days of the week.

What about answers
As the Romans passage quoted earlier makes clear, God's Spirit brings our requests into line with God's will. We have seen God answer our requests with a clear "no." When that has happened, the group has made a small protected place in which the pain of that answer and the move toward accepting it are shared. Face to face in a living-room, one sees one's own sorrow mirrored on a circle of other faces. The hands reaching out, the murmured prayers—how healing they are!

We have stood together at funerals, met in hospital rooms, and we have also gone to weddings that were "ours." We have rejoiced over babies and new jobs and we have prayed over engagements. God has answered according to his will. Sometimes it has been a clear "no," sometimes a resounding "yes." And often he has responded with "Wait. Trust me." God's people pray and God does things.

Summarizing, and adding to the list
1. Talk to God simply.
2. Be tender with people.
3. Be creative as you seek to help people learn to pray.

4. Make it a habit to thank God for answered prayer.
5. Begin to pray for needs throughout the week.
6. Be sensitive to the time spent in prayer.
7. Make a tradition of not allowing people to pray for their own requests.
8. Be conscientious about never discussing outside what is talked about inside the group.
9. Leaders: be willing to ask for prayer for yourselves.

Questions for study & discussion
1. Discuss an inspiring group prayer experience you have been part of. Try to analyze what made it special.
2. Discuss a frustrating group prayer experience you have had. Why was it frustrating?
3. On the basis of your discussion, go back to the summary of this chapter and add three suggestions to the list.
4. Join together to decide on rules for the people you are with, right now, that you think would enhance a time of mutual prayer. Some factors to consider:
☐ How many people will pray together?
☐ How long will they pray?
☐ Will the whole group give its requests to the smaller groups, or will each little group pray for its own needs?
☐ Will each person pray once, or is anyone free to break in?
☐ Are you going to kneel, stand, sit? Or does each person decide? Etc.
5. Pray, according to these personalized rules.
6. Come back together to critique your rules.

7
Relationships

The relationships within a small group ought to be moving in the direction of friendship. No one can make another person his friend. But as we practice Christianity we can be moving friend-ward toward each other. The Bible says so much about friendship that it becomes a specific text on the subject.

Friendship wreckers
"Gossip is spread by wicked people; they stir up trouble and break up friendships" (Prov. 16:28). How clear this is. It is unfriendly to gossip. Gossip wrecks friendships. In a small group a fabric is always being woven. It is a delicate fabric, constructed week by week with prayer, love, sensitivity, help from God, and truth. The name of the fabric is

trust. Without trust, openness is almost impossible. Without openness, needs are not known, and sharing is stifled. Without the knowledge of what the members of the group need and could share, where is the opportunity for growth? Gossip tears holes in trust.

"Violent people deceive their friends and lead them to disaster" (Prov. 16:29). Another friendship wrecker is the violent person. The Amplified Bible adds these words to the description of this person: "exceedingly grasping and covetous . . ." What are we to do if a very angry, greedy, or deceitful person comes to our group?

It seems from this proverb that the danger is in being his friend and being led by him while he is still violent. But we are not excused from showing him friendship. The company of a group of believers is an ideal place for God to begin to change such a person, if he is willing to change.

A violent person, whether his violence is shown in anger, or whether it comes from a greedy, covetous spirit that does violence to God's moral standards, needs to be accepted and dealt with some place, in order that the Holy Spirit can change him. The small group is a laboratory in which we rub against each other and share God's love and truth with each other and see ourselves and others changed.

We are watching God work his changes in two angry men. Two years ago we got a call from a young man we will call Roger, asking us to pick him up and drive him to our group. He had lost his license, was new in the area, and desired fellowship with other believers. We began taking him with us regularly to church on Sundays and to our group midweek.

We observed his deep love for Jesus Christ, and we also clearly saw his needs. He was lonely, quite a new believer, had had some trouble in his past, and was very afraid of slipping back into his old patterns. Although he longed to be able to relax, to accept hospitality and other practical loving help, he found it very difficult. Then he got into serious trouble with the law and was jailed for almost a year.

After a few months with good behavior, he was given permission to go to church and one of our young couples began picking him up every Sunday morning.

Then a new gentleman walked into our lives. We will call him Dan. Dan was directed to us by the pastor who had just introduced him to Jesus Christ. When he came to us he was a four-day-old Christian. Although he was very quiet during the study part of that first evening, he followed the lesson with great care in his Bible. Later, over coffee, he explained that he had been in the midst of a personal crisis so grave that he had turned to his daughter, who was a new believer, for help. She directed him to the pastor who then led him to Christ. His crisis, he told us, was the result of his violent temper, which was ruining his relationships.

Two violent men.

Dan came back the second week, full of joyful news about how God was at work in his family, healing relationships as he confessed his weakness and depended upon God to make him a man of peace.

As we finished rejoicing over Dan's good news, the conversation shifted and someone asked how Roger was doing. Win turned to Dan to explain who Roger was.

Win: "As I turned to Dan, my heart suddenly began to

pound. A possibility had just occurred to me. I leaned over to him, and murmured a name to him, 'Do you know Roger_____?' He flushed, nodded. 'Yes,' he answered, 'I arrested him.'"

Dan is the chief of police in the village where Roger had lived.

Dan thought for a minute and then said, firmly, "I'll write to him. I'll go see him."

Letters have now been exchanged between these two: the violent-tempered Roger and the violent-tempered Dan. God is making them more gentle. Part of the way he is doing this is through the small group.

The young couple who had been taking Roger to church didn't give up on him. Last year they kept going back to his apartment, taking him food and some articles of furniture he needed, after he had quit attending the group. He would not answer his door, but the couple kept trying. When they found he had been sent to jail, they asked for the privilege of going to pick him up every Sunday.

Now they and Roger are coming to church an hour earlier, as they are all taking instructions in church membership before the worship service.

Yesterday in church, we asked Roger: "How did you feel when you got your first letter from Dan?" His eyes filled with tears. Smiling, he answered quietly, "It was a lift, a real big lift." God put Dan in our particular group to give him a chance to minister to Roger, and to be supported by us as he did so.

Friendship enhancers
"If you want people to like you, forgive them when they wrong you. Remembering wrongs can break up a friend-

ship" (Prov. 17:9).

Some of us have been together in our group for seven-and-a-half years. At some point we have all disappointed, frustrated, and offended each other. Each of us has broken things, forgotten to do things. We *have* gossiped. We *have* been greedy and led each other astray.

If we are going to continue to practice being Christians, we have to forgive each other, and having forgiven each other, we have to quit remembering what we have forgiven.

The host home of a small group is so important to the atmosphere of the group. We have been fortunate. Our hosts constantly "forgive" us for coming every week. We are welcomed whole-heartedly. They do not appear to hang onto memories of the bugs we let in every summer and the snow we trample in each winter. The coffee is always ready when we come and the cups are washed after we leave, week in and week out.

They accept with grace the group members who come a bit early, to be nourished by the feeling of the family in residence. With love they pull another chair up to their dining table and share those minutes before everyone else comes through their front door.

"Friends always show their love" (Prov. 17:17).

Beginning to practice friendly, rather than unfriendly, behavior leads one into all sorts of difficulty. Who wants love shown to them now? Some people need a reassuring hand shake or hug. Others do not wish to be touched. Some people slip in the back door and sit out of sight. Others come in needing to be noticed as they come.

If we are going to begin and continue showing love, we need to *know* one another. This means that time must be built into the evening for relationships. The package marked "relationships" must never be left out of the evening. Oh, how dependent we must always be on God's Spirit to direct us to the division of time and the sensitivity to each person present!

Another proverb, Proverbs 27:14, speaks to this in a comical way: "You might as well curse your friend as wake him up early in the morning with a loud greeting." If your friend is an "owl," and you are a "robin" and you come singing by his window at dawn, toss gravel against his window and call out to him to join you in greeting the sun, he may treat your cheery good morning as a curse.

Showing love has to be done in a way the other person can respond to. We found this early in our marriage. Win, enjoying clothes herself, began giving Bob clothes for gifts. He hated that. Bob knew that any sensible person would count tools the choicest possible present, so he bought Win scissors and kettles. She hated that.

Down from the exquisitely sensitive Jesus, who knew to give Peter a nickname, through the leadership of a small group, out through all the people who come, the practice of discreet, enduring, forgiving, patient, friend-love must flow.

We cannot leave "Friends always show their love" without talking about the members of our group that we seldom or never get to see.

Our church has assigned missionaries to each neighborhood group. Our group has been assigned a couple in the Philippines and a single woman in Paris. We are asked not to consider these people as service or outreach relationships, but as people who are part of our group.

During our missions' conference each year, we are hosts to a missionary person, couple, or family for a special evening. We have dinner together as a group, spend the evening getting to know each other and praying with each other. These guests, while not officially "ours" in the sense of those assigned to us, often step into our hearts unofficially.

We are struggling to mature in the way we express our love to all our missionaries. Some, of course, we have never met. To say you "always show your love" to someone you have never seen, haven't prayed for, or written to in months, is an obvious lie.

Several years ago we began a pattern that has helped us to know and remember this part of our midweek family. As letters come from our missionaries, we put them in a manila envelope. When we have collected several of these letters, and shared the highlights with everyone, we hand them around for people to take home, read, and pass on.

Many of us have also committed ourselves to praying for them and their ministries one day a week. We have a sign-up sheet, and anyone who wants to can pick a day to pray for our missionaries.

And then, once a month, we have a delightful break in our routine called "Kids' Night." On this night, parents are invited to bring along their children ages four to ten. We all sit around the living room together, exchanging names and admiring important things like new shoes. We sing together, too, and after that Miss Shirley takes the children to another part of the house for a Bible lesson, memorizing, drama, singing.

In forty-five minutes to an hour we call them back to hear what they have learned. Then we have goodies together, visit some more, and everyone goes home.

But while Miss Shirley (a loving Christian day school

teacher and faithful member of our group) is teaching the children, we make a tape. We discuss one of our missionary persons or families, and how we are praying for them; we talk about what is happening with us; we sing—all on tape. And then we send the tape off to the missionaries.

So, slowly and clumsily, we are learning to show love to another part of our small group.

The disciplines of friendship
"The kisses of an enemy may be profuse, but faithful are the wounds of a friend" (Prov. 27:6 NIV). Yes, "friend-wounds" will be a part of the life of any group that is mutually committed to building up one another as part of the body of Jesus Christ.

The Bible instructs us to speak the truth in love, and a leader must sometimes speak truthfully, even though he knows that word of truth will be a wound. What will a leader do, for example, if someone in the group announces that he or she is getting a divorce because God told him to? What is the group to do if a course of action on the part of one of its members is announced, and it is wrong? There are times when to not give someone a friend-wound is to give, instead, an enemy-kiss.

"Iron sharpens iron; so a man sharpens the counten-ance of his friend" (Prov. 27:17 KJ). We need to risk chal-lenging each other, even as we remain sensitive to the thin line between hot discussion and angry arguments.

"No more lying, then! Everyone must tell the truth to his fellow-believer, because we are all members together in the body of Christ. . . . Do not use harmful words, but only helpful words, the kind that build up and provide what is needed, so that what you say will do good to those who hear you. And do not make God's Holy Spirit sad: for the Spirit is God's mark of ownership on you, a guarantee that the Day will come when God will set you free. Get rid of all bitterness, passion, and anger. No more shouting or insults, no more hateful feelings of any sort. Instead, be kind and tender-hearted to one another, and forgive one another, as God has forgiven you through Christ" (Eph. 4:25, 29-32).

Summary
Taking time to consider the value of friendships makes one aware of their preciousness. After studying the direction toward friendship as an ideal, and after noticing what the Bible says about friendship, our youth group wrote their own "friendship proverbs." We share a few of them with you here.

□ A friend is one who knows you as you are, understands where you've been, accepts who you've become, and still gently invites you to grow.

□ A friend hears the song in my heart and sings to me when memory fails.

□ A true friend stays and listens even after he wants to leave.

□ Finding a true friend is like peeling off sticks of celery to get at the heart of the stalk: each stick is another trial, and the friend that lasts through it is one step closer to being a true friend.

□ Friendship does not live by smiles alone but by everything that proceedeth out of the heart of both concerned.

□ A true friend seeks those whose hearts are cold, and sticks close until they melt.

Questions for study and discussion

We can learn much about friendship behavior by watching Jesus' actions in the Gospels. In John 1, he is just meeting the men who will be the closest to him. Read John 1:35-50, observing Jesus' matchless friendliness. Use the following questions as a basis for discussion:

1. Who does he put at ease? How?
2. How does he display the generosity vital to friendship?
3. He gives one man a nickname. Discuss his choice of the person and the nickname he gave him, in the context of building relationships.
4. Notice Jesus' Groups
5. Make a list of ideas from watching Jesus that would help "oil" the relationships in a new small group.

8
Reaching Out

As we have looked into the overall life of small groups, we have taken off the lid on worship, teaching, prayer, and relationships. If we were to stop there, we would be falling sadly short of the ideal. We would soon become ingrown and stagnant. To complete the balanced life of the group, we must reach out. We must serve.

The concept of service is central in Christian thought. Jesus left heaven for our needs. The adored chief ornament of heaven came to serve, rather than to be served. It is his attitude toward service that gives us our pattern.

The Word of God is saturated with the teaching that we are to serve God ("serve the Lord with gladness, come before his presence with singing"), and to serve one another ("serve one another in love"). And the New Testament makes it clear that God's Spirit enables every Christian to serve. He lives in us to give us a heart and sensitivity to serve, and he gives each of us gifts so that we have a particular area of ability in which to serve.

What is the small group's part?
Small groups, living-room-sized portions of the local church, are designed to facilitate both the preparation for and the practice of service. Everything that a healthy small group does together helps prepare its members for service and involves its members in service.

As people learn how to worship and then begin to worship, they are serving God. As they study the subject of prayer and begin to pray for one another, they are serving each other. As they build relationships of trust and share needs, opportunities for simple, homely service arise and are met. Exchanged baby-sitting, meals brought to a home, cookies brought to the midweek meeting, coffee plugged in, people listened to and comforted . . . all these are acts of service-in-love.

When the leader teaches the Bible, inviting participation so that issues are clarified and everyone's study skills are increased, he is teaching the theological foundation for service. Service, his hearers learn, is commanded, encouraged, and rewarded throughout the Bible. Service is what God's people do. Servants are what God's people are.

Small groups are ideal places for the discovery, development, and use of the particular abilities given to people in the group by the Holy Spirit. In the act of serving, in building up this mini-body of believers, one often finds in oneself abilities that in a larger group would have gone unnoticed.

Karen and Lynn arrived at our group for the first time on the same evening. Karen was longing for someone to teach. Her background had prepared her to teach bible and God had given her a desire to teach. Lynn is a very young Christian, much in need of being taught. In a group of twenty or so people, the need and the ability and desire to meet the need were discovered within a week or two. Now the girls are meeting weekly and both are growing.

What about the church, proper?

The church, proper, has an essential role to play in preparing its various parts to serve. In Ephesians 4:11-12 we read: "It was [Christ] who 'gave gifts to mankind'; he appointed some to be apostles, others to be prophets . . . others to be pastors and teachers. He did this to prepare all [of the rest of] God's people for the work of Christian service, in order to build up the body of Christ." The obvious teaching here is that the pastoral gifts are given to church leaders to prepare all of the rest of God's people to serve. so the preaching, teaching, administration, shepherding of the church staff is the starting point for the service training of its parts.

The church acts as a model for its small components. Its community and missionary concern and its care for its resident members demonstrate its servanthood philosophy to all who attend. It acts, too, as an information resource center: a place where its members can learn of opportunities for service.

The church is the logical place for small group leaders to be trained. In our church, leaders are appointed and trained by the church. There is a mandatory one-semester-long training class that each leader must complete. This class not only teaches the potential leader all sorts of useful skills, but having such a class requirement is a statement on the interrelationship between the church and its parts, and the seriousness with which the church takes the neighborhood groups.

Balancing responsibility and freedom

God always does his part. He has left us his Word, revealing that we are to serve him and each other. He has given us his Spirit to empower us to serve. He has given each of us gifts according to his will, to enable us to serve each other usefully in a particular area.

If the local church is doing its part in teaching, modeling, informing, and training small group leaders, what is left for the small group?

What is left for the small group is to find its way into a balanced outreach, welcoming and being obedient to service responsibilities that the church as a whole asks it to undertake, and yet remaining open and creative about its own service possibilities.

In this continuing adventure, led by God's Spirit through the church, individual or group circumstances, as well as the personal vision and gifts of the group members, we begin to serve.

Let's examine two very different styles of small group service.

Our group's service pattern: scattered!

Paul drives a hundred miles each way on Sundays, to teach the high schoolers in a Korean church. He discovered this opportunity on his own. He had some difficulty communicating with these young people and a real problem disciplining them in a helpful way. He brought these needs to our group and we began to pray regularly for him as he taught. He immediately noticed an improvement in his teaching and authority.

Judy reads to blind people in a rest home. She found this opportunity on her own. She tells us her experiences, both poignant and comical, and we listen and are intrigued. We pray for her.

When we told our group about this book, Debby offered to type it for us. She was already typing for Win as a service of love, and was willing to add the manuscript work. Of course, if she had not been in our group, she would not have known of this need.

Jerry and Deb were willing to teach the Bible study whenever we had to be away. Thus, they began to display some leadership abilities and also to show interest in other leadership opportunities. We told them about the leadership training class for group leaders. They took it, and decided that when the time was right they would ask to begin a new group. They stayed with our group for many months, as we prayed and talked and waited for God's time for us to have a "baby." Now they have been "parents" of a new group for a year. For months after they spun off, we began each of our evenings together by praying for the new group.

The list goes on: "Miss Shirley" of Kids' Night spends her summers traveling to rural communities to provide children in the midwest with week-long Bible schools. Lynne helps in the tape ministry of a community-wide women's Bible study. Dave has started a Bible study with

some of the men at his place of work. And the list continues, but we will stop, here.

In many of the serving ministries of our people, our
part is to be interested, to encourage, to pray. In others,
we have been the means of their having the opportunity
to serve, and in some instances, the group, itself, is the
object of the service.

John and Shirley's group's service: focused!

John and Shirley and their family have a house guest
ministry. They also lead a small group. In June of 1980,
their home was sheltering only their own family, and
they asked the Lord to show them who should be living
there with them. The following Sunday, at our church, a
pastor shared the need for sponsors for Laotian refugees.
John and Shirley, being made aware of the need, began
to pray and to share their concern with their group who
caught the concern and also began to pray. They invited
the pastor to speak. "As he outlined the need for a sponsor
and a support group for a family," Shirley recalls, "it
seemed the Lord had supplied us with everything needed,
including desire."

Within a month, papers were processed through a relief
organization, as the group continued to pray about the
selection of the family of God's choice. At the same time,
they were praying about the preparation of the hearts of
this family to be ready to receive the gospel. While they
prayed, they put together living quarters for the family in
John and Shirley's home, the group working shoulder to
shoulder to create a home within a home. They also spent
time studying materials on culture and related needs.

Shirley comments: "We were really unified in prayer,

realizing what a monumental event it was, but God gave us a great peace and many detailed assurances of his provision."

The Laotian family of seven arrived, without English, and with few possessions, but bringing with them lovely smiles and sweet spirits that gave the small group waiting to welcome them confidence that God had put them all together. For the two-and-a-half months that they lived in John and Shirley's home, the group members were in daily contact with them, for many hours a day. Medical procedures, school arrangements, shopping for necessities, planned family and family-group outings involved everyone.

Later, a missionary, speaking Laotian, was able to discover that the mother had desired to find God before she ever came to America. She shared with the missionary: "It was all dark to me, and now it is light. I understand." After further time with the missionary, she and her husband asked Christ to be their Saviour and Lord.

Suggestions for group leaders

Continue to contribute to the security of the members of your group. Feeling comfortable and cared for is an important prerequisite for the development of servant attitudes.

Encouraging service involvements, turning your group away from itself to reach out, is like opening windows in a stuffy room. Balance security and comfort with the challenge to risk and adventure. Expect people to reach out in service. Model a servant life style, yourself. Give the Holy Spirit room to work. Be ready to encourage and support ideas that you would never have thought of.

Ask God to help you keep a balance between freedom and responsibility between creativity and realism.

Reminders and other last thoughts

The small group is like a heart. Into the heart, midweek, struggle all the tired "blood cells" to get revitalized. Then, renewed, they go out to serve the living God and his people in his strength.

Having examined this last major component of activity of a growing small group, we hand the whole package, wrapped around with love and prayers, to anyone who may be called of God to take on the responsibility of helping a living-room-sized part of his church practice its Christianity.

Yours is not the lecture hall of the church, but the laboratory. You are not the "professor," but the "lab instructor." Yours is just a part of the work and life and outreach of the whole church, but it is truly a most important part.

John R. W. Stott, well-known Christian speaker and writer and retired pastor wrote recently: "Every healthy local church will have not only the united service of dignity on the Lord's Day, but will divide the congregation into fellowship groups, which meet in each other's homes during the week. We need both: we must not choose between them" (*Christianity Today*, June 12, 1981, p. 19).

"Instead, by speaking the truth in a spirit of love, we must grow up in every way to Christ, who is the head. Under his control all the different parts of the body fit together, and the whole body is held together by every joint with which it is provided. So when each separate part works as it should, the whole body grows and builds itself up through love" (Eph. 4:15-16).

Questions for study & discussion

In this chapter we have told you about two styles of service that small groups may be involved in: 1) individual service, supported by the group, and 2) a group service project.

Invite the people you are with to express themselves on what they individually would feel comfortable about being involved in. Then:

1. Ask each person to share the service that is part of his present life. (This may take some thinking through. Many very private, quiet deeds are done in the name of Christ.)

2. Are there those in your group today who have a vision for a group project? Something your church or community or a mission field needs?

3. If there is time, brainstorm. Imagine that you have decided to go with a group project. Ask people to share with everyone a Holy Spirit gift they have. Try to think what sort of group project the gifts present would make possible. Discuss the further training the gifts might need. What else would be necessary to make the project work? Money? Time? Release from present responsibilities?

4. What have you all learned through this discussion?

Appendix

2
James 1:1-18

Preparation

1. For your own benefit, evaluate the last lesson by writing a one-paragraph comment to yourself about the clarity of the teaching, use of time, evidence of God working, response of individuals. It would be helpful for you, the leader, to keep a small notebook or file folder for this study of James, including dates of your studies.

2. Continue to read the entire book of James daily, while you are studying the passage for this study, James 1:1-18. Think of a title that fits this passage.

3. After reading James 1:1-18 in a number of translations, note what James teaches about *trial, testing,* and *temptation* (or similar words in Bible paraphrases). In the Greek, the word for *testing* and *tempting* is the same; the meaning must be determined from the context. Summarize your understanding of James's teaching on the subject of testing/temptation so that you will be ready to help your group understand it.

4. Complete the exercises in the Member's Manual before the group meets. Doing this each week will help you grow and benefit from God's Word in James.

Bible Study

1. Pray aloud, asking God to help you understand what you read, and thanking him for his indwelling Spirit who makes it possible for believers to understand and obey what they read.

2. Read or have someone else read James 1:1-18 aloud. Ask group members to suggest a title for this portion of Scripture. Group members should discuss which title fits best, and write it in their manuals.

3. Explain that this is a lesson about the *results* of correct attitudes. All through these verses, James points out those good results, and in verse 12 he tells us that the person with correct attitudes is blessed. *Blessed,* here, means "happy, to be envied." We could say that James believes that the result of having correct attitudes is that we will be happy.

4. Ask group members to find Matthew 5:3-12, where Jesus is seen doing exactly the same sort of teaching. Read through a few of these Beatitudes.

5. Assign each subgroup (2-5 people) or individual *one* of the passages printed in the Manual. Use the directions under "Hear It!." When they have completed writing their Beatitudes, share all Beatitudes with the whole group. Give everyone a chance to copy all the Beatitudes into their Manual if they want to. (Sample Beatitude for verses 2-4: "Happy, to be envied, are those who face trials, for their faith will be developed into maturity.")

6. Read aloud James 1:13-18. Have the group discuss how James contrasts the good in our lives with the evil that comes when we give in to temptation. Compare their sources, their evidence, and their end results.

7. Ask two or three people to summarize the teaching from this lesson. Then give the group time to complete the "Live It!" section in their manual.

Plan for the Evening

■ *Fellowship*
Here's a suggestion for new or changing groups. When most people have arrived, ask everyone to get up and shake hands with three different people, greeting each person by name. Admit your own problem with remembering names, and encourage people to ask for help if they can't remember a name. The third pair to shake hands should sit together and take turns sharing an interesting/unusual/exciting/difficult thing that happened during the week. Each pair is to listen to each other without interruption and then ask and answer one question about what the other has said.

■ *Singing*
Sing together, using some of the songs and choruses you chose last week as theme songs for James.

■ *Bible Study*
Present the Bible study you have prepared.

Sample Lesson from Teacher's Handbook of *James: Hear It! Live It!*

■ *Worship*

After the lesson, ask two good readers to read Psalm 1 as a responsive reading, alternating verses. Ask the others to close their eyes and listen, making this a time to concentrate on God in worship.

■ *Prayer*

Ask members for prayer requests and answers to prayer. Encourage people to record prayer requests and answers, including the dates, in the prayer notebook at the back of the Member's Manual. If enough of your group is comfortable with praying aloud, you could ask for a volunteer to signify his or her willingness to pray for each request when it is given.

If your group has too few people comfortable with praying aloud, read the suggestions under "Getting Started" (p. 59) of the chapter on prayer in *Small Groups: Timber to Build Up God's House.*

Living-Room Tested Idea

When we taught this lesson, there were many new people in the group. Because we sensed they would feel uncomfortable formulating a Beatitude with others they didn't know, we revised our lesson plan. We still assigned subgroups (2-5 people to work together), but instead of sending them to different rooms to work, we had everyone stay in the circle. After each subgroup had suggested some of their own ideas, the entire circle gave additional ideas if they needed help.

2
James 1:1-18

Hear It! What is God saying to me?

Give a title for James 1:1-18. _____

_____

Put the teaching of each passage into the form of a Beatitude (see Matt. 5:3-12).

1. James 1:2-4: Blessed (happy, to be envied), is the one who

_____

_____

Sample Lesson from Member's Manual of *James: Hear It! Live It!*

2. James 1:5-8: Blessed (happy, to be envied), is the one who

_____

_____

*3. James 1:9-11: Blessed (happy, to be envied), is the one who

_____

_____

*You may want to make this Beatitude a two-part one.

Live It! How does God's Word apply to my life?

1. Look back to last week's lesson. How did you do on your commitment to read the book of James?

_____

2. Read over all the Beatitudes under "Hear It!" Choose one that focuses on an area where you would like God's help this week. Complete the prayer below, being very specific.

"Dear God, please help me this week, through the power of your Spirit, to begin to be a blessed person, as I trust you in the area of

_____

_____

I pray this in the strong name of Jesus Christ. Amen."
When you have written your prayer, pray it silently.

Prayer

Use the prayer notebook at the back of this Manual to record
dates of prayer requests and answers to prayer that the group
has shared.

Suggested Home Assignment

The following 7 psalms all contain "Blessed is the man who ..."
statements. Read the psalms, noting those statements that will
help you build a profile of a blessed, or happy, or to-be-envied
person.

Psalm 32 _____

Psalm 40 _____

Psalm 65 _____

Psalm 84 _____

Psalm 94 _____

Psalm 112 _____

Psalm 128 _____

■ *Time & place of next meeting:*

_____